Slip and Slide

by Jennifer Waters

Content and Reading Adviser: Joan Stewart
Educational Consultant/Literacy Specialist
New York Public Schools

Spyglass
BOOKS

COMPASS POINT BOOKS

Minneapolis, Minnesota

Compass Point Books
3722 West 50th Street, #115
Minneapolis, MN 55410

Visit Compass Point Books on the Internet at *www.compasspointbooks.com*
or e-mail your request to *custserv@compasspointbooks.com*

Photographs ©: Corbis/Chris Carroll, cover; Comstock, 5; Corel, 7, 9, 11, 13, 15, 17, 19.

Project Manager: Rebecca Weber McEwen
Editor: Alison Auch
Photo Researcher: Jennifer Waters
Photo Selectors: Rebecca Weber McEwen and Jennifer Waters
Design: Mary Walker Foley

Library of Congress Cataloging-in-Publication Data

Waters, Jennifer.
  Slip and slide / by Jennifer Waters.
      p. cm. -- (Spyglass books)
Includes bibliographical references (p.   ) and index.
  ISBN 0-7565-0241-1
  1. Winter sports--Juvenile literature. [1. Winter sports.] I. Title.
II. Series.
  GV841.15 .W38 2002
  796.9--dc21

                                 2001007325

Contents

Fun in the Cold

Just because winter may bring cold weather does not mean people have to stay inside! Many people enjoy ice and snow by building snowmen and playing winter sports.

Sledding

People ride sleds down
snow-covered slopes
or small hills.
Sledders have to be careful
not to run into trees,
other objects, or each other.

Sled

Stay Safe
Never wear a scarf when you are sledding. It could get caught under the sled.

Snowshoeing

Snowshoeing is a fast way
to walk or hike
through the snow.
Snowshoes help keep your feet
from sinking into deep snow.

Snowshoes

Skating

Ice skating started long ago as a way to travel from one place to another. *Hockey* first became a sport back around 1870. College students came up with the rules people use today.

Ice skates

Skiing

The fastest kind of skiing
is downhill skiing.
The **courses** are very steep.

In cross-country skiing,
the skier runs to glide across
the snow.

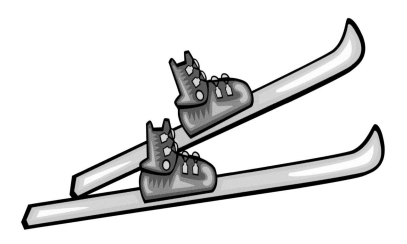

Skis

Snowboarding

Snowboarding started in the 1960s when some surfers decided to try surfing on the snow instead of on ocean waves.

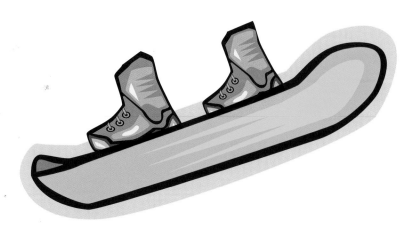

Snowboard

Snowmobiling

Snowmobiles are sleds with motors. They travel very fast over ice and snow. Riders are careful not to tip them over—especially when they are turning.

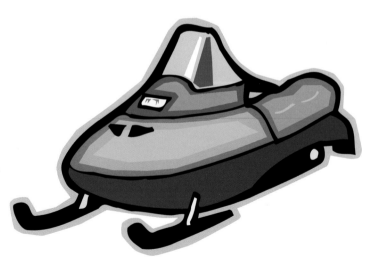

Snowmobile

Fun Fact
Snowmobile racing started in the
1960s as a race across open land.

Bobsledding

Bobsled teams have
two people or four people.
The team races its bobsled
down an icy *chute* that
is full of twists and turns.
The person in front steers.
The person in back
works the brake.

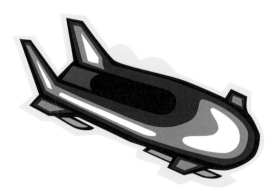

Bobsled

Fun Fact
Bobsleds can reach speeds over 100 miles per hour.

Winter Long Ago

1. Imagine you live in a cabin in the snowy woods. Cars and snowmobiles have not been invented yet.

2. Write about how you get around on the snow and ice. Where would you need to go and why?

3. Draw a picture of your favorite way to get around.

Glossary

chute—a long tube that things can slide down

course—the path someone follows from start to finish in a race

gates—poles or flags that skiers ski around

hockey—a sport played on ice where teams of six players try to score points by hitting a hard, round disk into a goal

slalom—a ski course that winds back and forth between gates or flags

Learn More

Books

Maass, Robert. *When Winter Comes.* New York: Henry Holt, 1993.

Ruis, María. *Winter.* New York: Barron's, 1998.

Stone, Lynn M. *Antarctica.* Chicago: Childrens Press, 1985.

Web Site

Brain Pop
www.brainpop.com/science/seeall.weml
(click on "seasons")

Index

GR: F
Word Count: 215

From Jennifer Waters

I live near the Rocky Mountains.
The ocean is my favorite place.
I like to write songs and books.
I hope you enjoyed this book.